1

LET "OUR" TRUTH BE TOLD

SHORT NARRATIVES
FROM THE HEART, MIND, BODY AND
SOUL
OF "WOMEN" GLOBALLY

By: Valerie Golden Allen
& Contributors

LET "OUR" TRUTH BE TOLD

SHORT NARRATIVES:
FROM THE HEART, MIND, BODY, AND SOUL
OF "WOMEN" GLOBALLY

VJ

PUBLISHING HOUSE, LLC.

Let "Our" Truth Be Told

Short Narratives: From the Heart, Mind, Body and Soul of "Women" Globally

Published By:

VJ PUBLISHING HOUSE, LLC.

20451 NW 2nd Avenue Suite 112 Miami Gardens,
Florida 33169
United States of America

2022, VJ Publishing House, LLC. All rights reserved.
ISBN: 978-1-939236-16-6

COPYRIGHT: 2022 Valerie Allen
EDITED BY: VJ PUBLISHING HOUSE, Editing/Revision Team
COVER & INTERIOR DESIGN: WILDLING GRAPHICS, Lisa Lawrence

PRINTED IN THE UNITED STATES OF AMERICA
THIS BOOK IS PRINTED ON ACID-FREE PAPER.

Contributors

Durrell Sykes (St. Petersburg, Florida)

Loreta Costanza (Argentina, Mendoza)

Tiquana Deloach (Miami, Florida)

Lucretia Williams (Newark, New Jersey)

Ivy Asumadu (Ghana, Kusami)

Trenda Dorsey (Miami, Florida)

Patti Mason (Antigua, Virgin Islands)

Chaunquavia Manuel (Carol City, Florida)

Vera Ofori (Ghana, Kusami)

Panitra Jackson (Miami, Florida)

Bonita Peaches Davis (Los Angeles, California)

Laquisha Williams (Nassau, Bahamas)

Valerie "Golden" Allen (Miramar, Florida)

I dedicate this literary work to every woman of "Purpose..."
With Prayer, Praise, and Perseverance, you will defy the odds; they are in your favor.
And that's the TRUTH!

Valerie Golden Allen

Acknowledgments
Valerie 'Golden' Allen

I honor God for giving me the vision and direction to bring forth this transparent literary work. I am grateful for the women contributors (Durrell, Laquisha, Lucretia, Loreta, Vera, Ivy, Trenda, Patti, Tiquana, Bonita, Chaunquavia, Panitra) who found it not robbery to share their "TRUTH" experiences so eloquently with the world. Blessed beyond measure, despite the challenges they have faced, these women define strength and resilience. They have a robust faith that has sustained them through tumultuous and challenging times. These relentless women of stature are indicative of God's Amazing Grace, Mercy, and Power. In the times that we're living and situations that have knocked at doors personally, I hope you find a layer of hope to persevere in your quest for life after reading their "Truths."

With every fiber of myself, I appreciate the support and love of countless individuals who cheered me on when it seemed as if I wouldn't make it to the finish line. To my amazing parents, that are now watching over me, I never could have made it without your love for my siblings and me. I believe I've made you proud, Mama & Daddy, and all of it was worth it. To my children, Victoria, Vernon, Veronica and Valencia, you are now my earthly pillars of strength. What a joy knowing that God trusted me to birth and carry you through life thus far. You are "MY VICTORY!" My beautiful grandchildren, family, friends and supporters near and far, simply THANK YOU!

Over the years, I've had the opportunity to encourage, empower, and enrich the lives of many. Some were in a storm, headed for one, or coming out of one. My mission is evident, and my revelation is correct that my Spirit is in synch, and I've finally figured out this thing called LOVE. Indeed, it does conquer all. Lastly, I pray that every woman can take something from these "Truths" and apply them to their life and find their way to freedom. Happy Reading! Peace…

THERE IS A FREEDOM IN TRUTH!

SOJOUNER TRUTH
(Women's Rights Activist)

We Hold These Truths...

The Truth Will Set You Free!
Valerie Golden Allen

FACE YOUR TRUTH...

DURRELL SYKES

MY TRUTH

Not all fairytales end with "and they live happily ever after". Some end with what seems like a nightmare you can't wake up from. At least, that was the case with me after my divorce.

I thought I would be married forever and a day...we would work hard, building a (small) family, put our children through college, retire and grow old together. Then I woke up one day and realized that it would not happen. I was married at age twenty-five, my son was born when I was thirty, and by age thirty-two, I divorced. I thought to myself; surely I will be married again in a few short years; after I heal and regroup. I told myself you're decent looking, have a degree and several years of work experience; I provide for myself, know how to maintain my responsibilities, love family, and love being married. There was no doubt in my mind that God also wanted me to be married, which is why He created Adam and Eve (for relationship) and instituted the marriage covenant. Although I needed time to heal from some things, I also needed time to nurture my son, mold him into a productive, responsible young man, and teach him how to treat women. In my analytical brain, this should not have taken forever...but in my mind, it seems as if it did.

My mother passed when I was twenty-seven. As time passed, the years of being a single woman went into decades. I can't say that I was a "single mother" because, although divorced, my ex-husband and father of my son were alive during this time, plus I had an incredible Village of family members who were there for me whenever I needed them. Being the youngest of my siblings and the last to have children, I was grateful to have the support of so many.

I spent the decade of my thirty's trying to find my way as a Mother and in Ministry. Balancing family and faith and fulfilling my obligations in my home and the House of God was challenging. In the area of relationships, I dated here and there, but nothing too serious. I was challenged by my father's death, not wanting to bring the men I dated around my son to avoid relationship bonding (in case it didn't work out). Not to add, I had fiery trials to pass thru with my ex-husband, who had married a demon seed. Therefore, I spent years in spiritual warfare to keep my son safe and myself sane. I came out stronger and a little wiser. I matured in many ways when I reached forty but found myself entangled. Out of all the men I had dated…some were low-number millionaires, some were in positions of authority, and others were not as outgoing but led very productive lives and were well off financially. However, there was one, we were not from the same place but grew up in homes where neither of us was afraid of hard work nor afraid to build. He was charismatic, a smooth talker, personable, and did well for himself. In all honesty, that was the problem; he was only concerned about himself. It matters not how well a person can put up a good front; our true colors will always come thru because we can only be "Great Pretenders" for so long. You may ask why I was in it for so long. There were seasons when I dated other men, and there were also seasons when I was led to believe that we would get married and build the life we both wanted. After numerous emotional roller-coaster rides, the on-again-off-again is we, or ain't we gonna be together, was draining. I finally released him to do whatever he wanted. I finally did what I knew but refused to because I didn't want to be single again. The reality was that I was single the whole time.

When I reached fifty, I was more confident than ever before. I dealt openly with my emotions and separated the facts from the fairytale lies. No longer was my heart a swayed swing. In September 2019, I was appointed and accepted to Pastor a church. In January 2020, I had an Installation Celebration which consisted of church members, family and friends, and men and women in Ministry from all over. One of the Pastor's visiting the South Florida area was invited and came as a guest. Ironically, he would fill in for one of the pastors who were a no-show. After the celebration, I thanked the visiting stranger (to me), and we exchanged short talk. I had a lot of guests to greet, and he did not wish to stay for my V.I.P. reception.

Approximately three months later, the CV-19 pandemic overwhelmed the globe, and life as we knew it was forever changed. Social Media pages had become the obituary section for all to discover who had succumbed to the deadly coronavirus. Millions of lives were lost from March 2020 to July 2021 due to CV-19 and its complications. As some quarantines started to lift gently and outdoor activities were allowed or encouraged because being indoors for so long had caused bouts of depression, more people were venturing safely to water sports and recreational activities. I just happened to be on Facebook when I saw a picture of the visiting Pastor who came and participated in my pastoral celebration service, out on a day trip enjoying a lovely day. I graciously commented, "Hello, Sir." He In-Boxed me on Messenger, and initially, I ignored it because most of the messages that come thru my In-box are foolishness. I thought to myself; he doesn't know you like that, so get over yourself; he's only speaking to you. I replied with a short message and told him the best time I could talk, and we exchanged phone numbers.

When we connected, I explained to him that the best way to reach me was by cell. We got caught up on all things family, Ministry, and CV-19 people who were dear to us and had passed away.

He said, "Do you mind if I ask if you're seeing someone?"

Chuckling, I replied, "No," and asked myself, where did he get that from?

He then said, "I thought you would be married by now because when I inquired about your status at your celebration, I was told you would be married soon, but when I checked your Facebook status, it says you're single."

Hmmm... that's strange as I laughed out loud and said emphatically, "Very single."

He then asked, "Excuse my straightforwardness, but we're both adults. Do you mind if we get to know each other? Is that something you would like?"

Blushing, I replied, "Sure. I don't see why not."

After that, we talked at least three times a day. The things we discovered we had in common were scary. For example, our birthdays are a day apart; we love being near water; our churches have the same name, and we're both Pastors. Last but not least, we both wanted to be married again. Both of us gave clarity. We didn't just want to be married, but we wanted to be married to the right person or the person God wanted us to be with.

As we approached the middle of July, he asked if he could take me on a date near the water so that we could hold hands while walking on the beach and get to know each other. Being analytical, I began to wonder how it would or could happen because we live approximately three hours from each other.

He picked up on my reluctance and said, "You're trying to figure out how I will make this happen. That's not for you to worry about; I asked you out, so let me take care of the details. All I need is your consent."

Chuckling as I often did from his humor, I replied, "Okay then; yes, you can take me out."

We arranged a weekend for him to return to South Florida and a couple of places we would dine. Our first date was a double date on a Friday night with his Sister-Cousin and her fiancée. She had also accompanied him to my installation celebration service, but we didn't have a chance to meet then. He had roses waiting for me, which happened to be the same color pink as my dress. The restaurant's ambiance was casual and cozy, and the Cuban food was some of the best I'd ever had in South Florida. Our conversations were about family, our parents, and childhood memories that we will never forget. We became so engaged in our laughter that we didn't realize the place was closing. As we looked around, we saw the employee cleaning up around us. We were the last ones left in there. Sunday's date was over brunch; we met up at a place on Hollywood Beach. His wish was mine to honor, and we did go walking near the water after we ate. He left South Florida around 3:00 pm, returned home, and talked about most of his long-distance drive.

I then liked talking to and being with this seasoned young man. He was naturally funny, like a natural comedian, but only truthful. His rawness made me laugh harder because it was authentic and reminded me of my mother. His mild mannerism reminded me of my Dad. All jokes aside, the flipside of the mildness was a Beast! Approximately three months passed, and we'd been in each other's presence on several occasions. We shared our painful pasts and the disappointment of spending time (years) with great pretenders. On both ends, we welcomed transparency, and no matter how challenging it was to hear, we made each other comfortable so that each could share and have a safe space to communicate without being judged. Only spending valuable time helped us see the best in each other when others had chosen to see the worst. We prayed individually and knew that God had ordained our paths to cross the way they had. Neither of us could believe it was finally happening.

We had finally found love in its rarest and most genuine form. The nightmare of never marrying again seemed like it would never end and was about to be over. No pretense, lying to impress, no other persons (male nor female) to compete with, just the two of us. Our private engagement came in October 2021, and in December, we publicly announced our plans for marriage to our family and closest friends. We planned our intimate ceremony for March 2022, over the December holiday season. Due to CV-19 still affecting our lives, just in a less devastating way, we planned with the well-being of ourselves and our loved ones. Our Honeymoon was a 5-day cruise, and I moved to Northwest Florida upon returning to South Florida. Almost every day, God reveals why I had to wait nearly thirty years to marry again (from when I married the first time). Now I can see why none of those other relationships worked out.

God surprised me wonderfully and amazingly when I thought it would not happen. I was a Lady In Waiting… waiting on God and not man, to fill the void I felt in wanting to be with and belong to my Husband. Only God knew how badly I needed someone who wanted to be my earthly Provider, Protector and offer me peace of mind in knowing he was very present. My waiting on God meant I had to take myself off the (emotional) roller-coaster with other men, who only wanted to keep me wondering and guessing if we were or were not going to seal the deal. Waiting on God meant I had to be content with myself and embrace all the things I denied, like my areas of challenge and/or shortcomings. I had to wait for God to show me that I was still valuable, priceless, and worth being found and fought for. In my waiting on God, I became liberated! My wait brought me someone who was not afraid of my painful past, but rather, his love covered me, and it felt good! The love of God delivered me of insecurities that once held me back from being my best self. Just as there were no words to describe the pain of disappointment, there are no words to describe the joy of witnessing the miraculous power of (God's) love thru another human being. I am beyond ecstatic that I was a **"Lady In Waiting"** for God's best for me!

LORETA COSTANZA

NUGGET OF TRUTH

I arrived in the United States of America at the tender age of eight, as my mother and father were seeking a new life and opportunity. I thought I knew where we were going… but did not realize I was leaving my country of birth, Argentina, for a while. I knew it was a significant change, and I was excited as my mother told me, "We are hopping on an airplane to Miami!" The hot air as we stepped out of the airport, I still remember it… I knew no English, but I was enrolled at school. I remember not understanding what the teacher or students told me and feeling left out. My mother and father worked all day and tried to learn English. When it was homework time, one worksheet would take us three hours to complete using a dictionary. Luckily, as a kid, I was able to merge and start learning English quickly; I thank my ESOL teacher Mrs. Chippy for that. I did not know much about American culture, but slowly I was becoming an American myself; eating French Fries and Chicken Nuggets was my daily lunch.

The American dream ended when we were denied our visas five years after we arrived and had to move to Spain. I guess God knows what he does because this helped my little sister speak and write the Spanish language since she was already more advanced in English than me. It was a life change, from the language to the city life to everything being closed on Sundays. I liked it, but I begged to come back. A year after, I got my wish, and before I knew it, I was back in Miami, starting my first year of high school.

I became an adult at age eighteen when I graduated high school. With so many opportunities, I went to college and the university and graduated with my teaching degree. In little but no time, I was shaping the lives of many little children. This moment was demanding but rewarding for me as I knew the difficulties children can have in school and the hardships that shape a student's daily life. What I did not realize… is how to be a parent, but I would say that this career is shaping me into what I should or should not do with my future children. Engaging in my teaching career took a lot of courage and energy, as, towards an ending workday, I felt my ears ringing and could not turn on the radio while going back home.

I still managed to enroll in a gym, where my best friend and I made an effort to find ourselves doing heavy lifting, running, and even boxing. The more we went to the gym, the more this African American social guy spoke to me. He had a partner, and I minded my business, forcing myself to put a shield over someone who could break my heart… again. To "Tell the Truth," I had built a wall for myself from men… you see, they were never loyal to me, and I could not take that again. But somehow, I liked the chocolate man I saw at the gym. Before long, we would be boyfriend and girlfriend, as he ended his one-year miserable marriage… from an American woman to a Hispanic. My friends, this began the journey of learning what being an American is. One, two, three years down, and I had learned so much from him, oh how different our cultures are, from eating fried chicken wings and collard greens with hot sauce and every spice you can imagine… to getting his Starbucks every morning with two pumps of caramel. Those cultural differences turned out to be rather interesting yet, at times, challenging. However, we continue to embrace each other's upbringing.

As the relationship blossomed, we thought about expanding our family. You see, he is seven years older than me… and so we did. I was excited but scared at the same time. So many tests and doctor appointments, I pretended I did not care, but I really did…and again, I was afraid. I'm beginning to understand and embrace how wonderful it is to live in this country. I remember getting the call that day, and it was not a good one. "Your exam came out positive," but positive for what, I asked? Trisomy 13. I did not know what it was…but when I googled it, the words "Down Syndrome" hit me like a ton of bricks. You see, 1 in 200 pregnant women can be diagnosed with this extra chromosome. I did not know how to react, but I knew this was not okay. I did what my heart told me to; it was not easy, but before I knew it, I was not pregnant anymore, and life continued as if nothing had ever happened.

That part was just "SO" hard for me. How could I continue as if it did not happen? Should I have made another choice? Is it possible not to feel guilty as I do? "To Tell the Truth" it was one of the hardest things in my life. I researched and read that many couples go through this… I tried to heal with prayers, outdoor activities, and traveling. And seven months after, on a trip to Atlanta, my pregnancy test said pregnant again. This time I was not scared; my feelings were all excited. I knew this was my time to become a mom. My healthy boy is two years old today… terrible two's, they say… and yes, It's true.

"My Truth" is not as exciting as other people's, but the message I received from God is that timing is everything and "All things work for the good." I may or may not have another child…but I trust in God and his decisions because when the right things come to you, and the timing is correct, they will happen for you.

You are worth it. You are important and can overcome anything! Believe and love yourself, and never let your guard down.

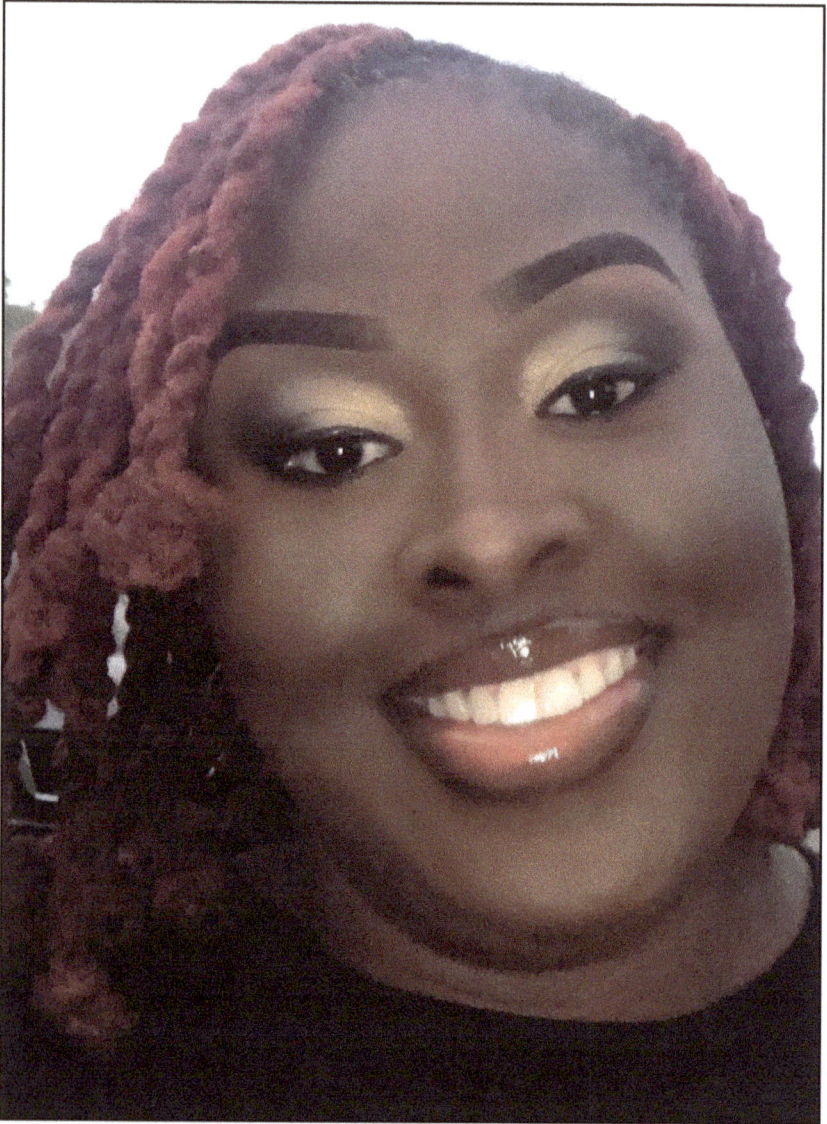

TIQUANA DELOACH

THE GOD HEAVEN TRUTH
"Seasons Change"

There is a season (a time appointed) for everything and a time for every delight and event or purpose under heaven—Ecclesiastes 3:1

Family is the most important thing besides God that you should always cherish. I grew up in a broken and dysfunctional home that taught me many life lessons and how to survive in struggles. I watched my grandparents work hard to ensure my siblings and I were cared for. I always promised myself that I would do the same when I got a family. Life was good for my family and I until the season changed. I had to renew my lease with the housing authority and was asked by my case manager if I was married. I replied yes, and she began to ask me questions about my husband and his background. I told her the **Truth**. She said I would not put him on the case because you would lose your housing. I thanked God that she was willing to help us out.

For years, everything was well until one of the employees gave my case to the housing manager, and she discovered I was married. My life began to shift, and I received a call to come to the office for a meeting. When I arrived, the lady started to interrogate me with questions about my husband and his criminal background. Finally, she said he wasn't qualified to be added to my case because of his past situation. She said I had two choices: kick him out and pay the fine to stay on the program or terminate my housing. My mind was racing because I knew I wasn't leaving my husband, and I didn't have the money to pay the fine either. I asked her whether she could give me a few days to decide. I just began to pray to God and ask Him for direction. The Holy Spirit said to tell the **Truth** and leave. At that moment, I was a little afraid because I didn't know what was next; I realized that my integrity meant everything to God, and if He told me to give it up, He had something better for me.

A few days later, I called the case manager and went into the office to sign the termination paperwork. The case manager looked at me the whole time like I was crazy and then asked if I was sure. I was at peace in my heart, but my mind was going a thousand miles a minute; I politely said to her yes, I'm sure. I couldn't believe what I was doing, but I knew what I did was right. She gave me thirty days to leave. Those were the longest days ever that we had to experience. I called everyone I knew, and no one had room for us. My husband had a place to go, but his family was concerned about me and vice versa. It was heartbreaking to know that no one was there to help when you're at your lowest place. I was very upset and felt betrayed because we always opened our home to anyone in need, and to see the favor wasn't returned was devasting.

Thirty days later, on July 1st, 2008, we had to turn the keys in to the landlord. I was on edge because I hadn't gotten a secure place for our kids. **"Packing and Praying"** was our model that day. My husband tried his best to stay calm and not go out and do something stupid to get money. My husband's uncle came over to help us move, not knowing our situation, and asked do we have a place to live. My husband told him he didn't want us to be a burden on anyone. His kind uncle opened his heart and offered for us to stay with him and his girlfriend. We put all our items in storage and went to his house.

We stayed there for almost two months until his girlfriend went to jail, and her family told us we had to leave. From there, we went to live with my mother-in-law. It was around the end of August, and school was starting for the kids. My husband worked labor pool jobs while I stayed home with our baby son Isaiah so our kids could have school clothes. Daily we called for assistance, and no rooms were available. Every day I prayed to God to move us to a better place; it was hell living with his mom, and every time my husband left, I would have to hear her talk badly about us to her friends. I couldn't take it anymore, but I didn't have any other solution.

One day, I was doing my hair and needed my scissors, so I asked his mom for them. Suddenly, she started yelling at me, so I got mad and walked away. She came and told me I needed to leave. I said okay and began to pack my clothes, and my husband so happened to come in simultaneously. He asked what was going on, and they got into an argument, and he started questioning me, asking me what I said to her. I told him I didn't say anything and that I was leaving to go to my grandma's house. I was furious because I didn't do anything and started crying. God told me before I left to apologize. I was questioning God because I felt she should be apologizing to me. I obeyed God. She looked at me with her family around her like she was the victim. My husband's sister came over and asked what happened, and his mom said she told me to go and my husband to stay. She started arguing, telling her mom why you are trying to separate them by kicking her out and wanting him to stay. My husband began to pack his belongings too, and we all left and went to my grandma's house.

The same headache I went through at my mother-in-law's house is the same thing my husband went through at my grandmother's house. My mom, who was living with my grandmother at the time, will constantly aggravate us about when we were leaving and that she didn't want to hear kids running around all day. To keep the peace, we would come there late at night and sometimes sleep in our car because my mom would be in the house telling us we couldn't come in so that she could get high with her boyfriend.

November 2008 was our day of getting away from all the drama and getting accepted into the Chapman Homeless Shelter. We had been calling every day, and finally, we got in. They tried to separate us upon arrival because they said men couldn't sleep in the rooms. But my husband and I began to pray because there was no way we were allowing anyone to separate us. The shelter coordinator saw us praying and told my husband she could make an exception. God touched her heart, and we were in the room together.

My relationship with God grew stronger during our stay, and I asked the Lord why we had to go through so much. He said I am breaking pride off. I didn't understand because I felt I had no pride issues, but God knows what my husband and I needed in that season. We were able to look at life and began to examine ourselves and the people around us. Often during testing time, God begins to reveal where you error. He knows what adjustments you need to be in right standing. God's hand was on us, and he showed Himself mightily while we were in our low place.

In February 2009, God blessed me with a job working at the Miami Beach Convention Center, which allowed me to save money. Eventually, we moved out of the shelter into a two-bedroom apartment in Little Haiti. A week later, my husband was blessed with a job at IHOP. Everything was starting to look bright, and our children were happy to be in their new place.

A year passed by, and another test hit. I was driving to the store with my second oldest son and my cousin, and smoke was coming from under the car's hood. I kept moving, and suddenly, I saw a spark of fire and immediately pulled over. I saw the smoke growing rapidly, and God said get out now. I grabbed the kids, got out of the car, and walked toward the sidewalk. The fire started blazing from under my hood. Then the whole front of my car was in flames. I was devasted, yet I thanked God at the same time because He spared our lives. Then the following week, my husband got laid off from his job, and my job started cutting hours because there were no events to work. We started getting behind on our bills, and before we knew it, the landlord put the eviction notice on our door. We left all our belongings outside the apartment and only took our clothes and personal things.

It felt like we were repeating the same cycle but in a different way. I called family members and people at the church in desperation not to have to relive being homeless again, and no door was opened except for my mother-in-law. She said she would allow us to come to stay there until we got on our feet. I sucked up my pride and went there, and she apologized to us, which broke many barriers and walls I had up towards her. I was hesitant at the time because of our past experience, but I knew God was up to something. My husband and I went through tough times in our marriage because the weight of struggling became overwhelming. I remember feeling like giving up on our marriage and just going on with life, but God didn't want us to separate.

Time passed, and I started desiring to spend time with my mom, not knowing why, but the desire came. I went to see her, and for some apparent reason, she had this big smile and was eager to tell me she had gone back to church and was getting into a drug program. I was thrilled to hear the good news and thanked God because I always prayed that my mom would get off the streets. Weeks later, on a Sunday afternoon, on October 3rd, 2010, I received a phone call from my grandmother that my mom had been murdered. I was already lying down because I had a headache and couldn't understand what my grandmother was saying, so I laid back down. My sister called, and when she called, I knew something was wrong; she said Tonya, which is what we called our mom, had gotten shot by Robert, her boyfriend. I jumped up and ran because I couldn't believe what I had heard. I thought for a split second that I was dreaming until I got to the crime scene and saw the yellow tape, and they were carrying my momma out in a body bag. I was hurt but couldn't feel pain because I didn't know my mom like I desired to know her. I couldn't sleep that night because I wanted to know what had happened and why. All I did was pray and cry out to God. The scripture says weeping may endure for a night, but joy comes in the morning.

My season of weeping was over, and I could now see the rainbow at the end of the tunnel. My husband got two jobs working as a cook for the University of Miami and as a stock clerk at Kmart. We already had money saved while staying with his mom, which allowed us to move into our new apartment. We moved into a one bedroom apartment and were content until God blessed us with a three-bedroom a year later.

God took our tragedy and allowed us to triumph over every obstacle and hindrance against us. I believe if He did it for us, He could do it for you. He has no respectable person and will move miraculously for His children. God has a way of blessing you when you least expect it.

LUCRETIA WILLIAMS

TRUTH OF THE MATTER

It was a warm summer evening, and I accepted a date to go out with a friend from college. We dined, danced, and reminisced on past events from school. It was a fun evening until "The Attempted Rape."

I was wondering why this is happening to me. My mind raced as I struggled to free myself. With my muffled screams and intense resistance, I escaped the clutches of my attacker and ran for my life. Due to this trauma, my life changed instantaneously. My mind was in a constant whirlwind of confusion, leading me to struggle with self-doubt for years and wonder what I did wrong. This is my story of "Redemption"…**The Resurgence Of "Me!"**

I sometimes cry, reflecting on what was and why I allowed certain people to take residence in my life. I was living this dream, hoping that this was not another failure. I spent much of my life hiding in the shadows without direction. How did I get here? There was no GPS as I struggled to find my way. With my desire to find true love and be loved, I gave much of myself to what I thought was love, even the wrong type of love, to almost losing myself. "Truth of the Matter," low esteem had me thinking I was not good, pretty, or intelligent enough. I realized that I was the means to satisfy whatever needs they wanted. With this state of mind, I accepted behaviors from others that are usually not tolerated. I became a dead person walking, only existing, never realizing my full potential… I was broken. They saw my capability and stole my self-worth. The habitual cheating, lies, and disappointments had me spiraling down into the abyss…I was hurting! Why didn't they see my value? "Truth be Told," neither did I. I might never receive the answers to these questions, so I write to be healed and hopefully set free. All I ever wanted was to build stability in a relationship.

Relationship, doesn't that embody two people? I was out of control, spiraling down this tumultuous black hole called life. I was depressed, confused, and unsure of my tomorrow. The need to break free of this pain felt like a noose wrapped around my neck. I was strangling… I struggled to breathe. According to Webster's

Dictionary, a relationship is how two or more concepts, objects, or people are connected. With this definition, I wasn't too far off in my thinking. However, I was off on what the other person's viewpoint was. So, this explains this loneliness that seems to creep up on me from time to time. In retrospect, I became a part of the problem because I condoned that behavior. I now realize I cannot change one iota of time, but I can forge forward with my life and free myself of the pain, shame, and shackles of my past.

The healing of the mind, heart, and soul is a journey. Reliving my past led me to journal for over a year. I sometimes wake up at two or three in the morning to write my innermost thoughts, remembering; you cannot do this, you cannot do that, and you are not good enough! Those words from my youth constantly came back to haunt me. Those words were the vein of my existence and set the course of me not believing in myself and being afraid to commit because of the fear of failure. There was so much grief and pain bottled up inside me that it started bursting out at the seams. I was reliving those moments again. Everything was flashing before me. I wanted to shut down and stop thinking, but my mind said, "NO," it is time to LIVE!!! "WHEN YOU SEE THE LIGHT, WALK THEREIN." Listen, never allow your light to flicker or be dim by anyone. There were times the process was so painful, but I had to dig deep into the depths of my core, regurgitating all that had taken refuge inside me. I was sick and did not know it. Something had to change, and it began with me! This struggle is real, but with each passing moment, each passing day, the load becomes lighter and tolerable. I was finally releasing the toxins to absorb life again. Through this enlightenment, I realize this will be a lifelong process. I understand a change needed to occur within me. My way of thinking; can no longer be misguided. I will become purposeful and not powerless. I'm reminded of Maya Angelou's words, "But still I rise. "I rise to hope, freedom, and a sound mind. Finally, I am rising to "Me."

"Truth Of the Matter" Being told as a child what I could not do and will never be, had my mind in bondage. But with daily affirmations and the assurance that I am more than a conqueror, I led the way for the resurgence of "Me." I will love myself with all my flaws, forget the past and wrap my arms around the future. I discovered this quote from "Simple Life": Do not be anyone's Down-Time, Spare-Time, Part-Time, or even Some-Time. If they cannot be there for you all "The Time," then they're not worth "Your Time!" This quote speaks volumes. It is befitting for "This Time" as I walk in my newfound power of self-love.

"Truth of the Matter" it's suitable for All-Times!" Today is a new day, and I have discovered love within and regard for my well-being and happiness. I "NOW" know that I am blessed beyond measure. No longer am I oppressed! I am walking in my "TRUTH," knowing I'm fearfully and wonderfully made! As I close, I would be remiss not to honor my God, who reached down and pulled me and my thoughts out of the biles of HELL. He is my "Way Maker and Redeemer!" His name is JESUS!!! I am the Apple of His eye, and He loves me unconditionally! He opened my heart, mind, body, and soul to see the tumultuous life I was living and replaced it with His limitless "LOVE," and I will be forever grateful. Listen, Reader; there is no greater love than God's.

In closing, "Truth of The Matter" brokenness does not have to be a life sentence. When your eyes open, stay woke and follow your path of Redemption. Listen, every fragment in your life can be made whole and render you complete again…I am a testament to that! Finally, I am ready to open my heart to give love and be LOVED!!! No longer lost, I finally found ME!

YOUR DEEPEST THOUGHTS

Which "Truth" can you relate to?

_____
_____
_____
_____
_____

What will you do now that you've faced the Truth?

_____
_____
_____
_____
_____

What plan of action will you develop to move forward as you walk in your Truth?

_____
_____
_____
_____
_____
_____
_____
_____

SPEAK THE TRUTH...

MAYA ANGELOU

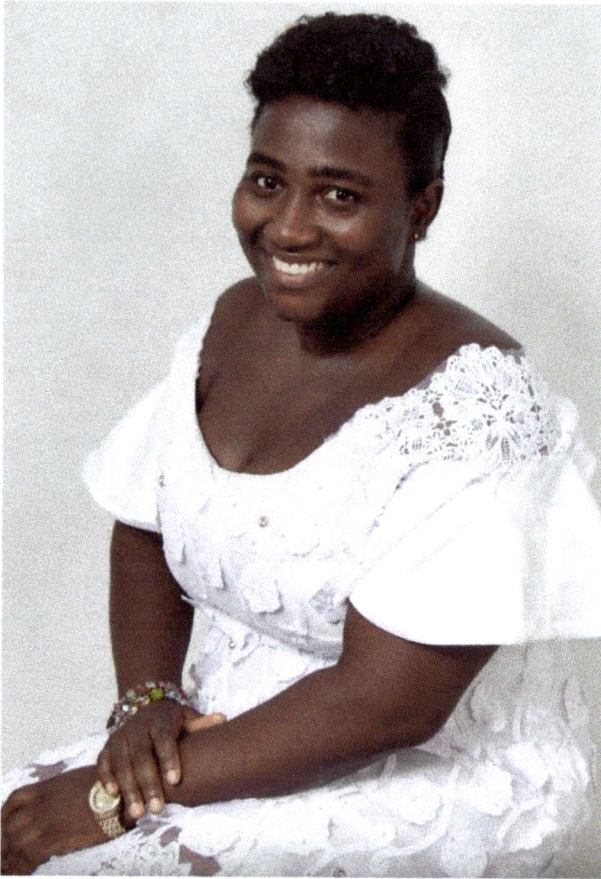

IVY ASUAMADU

BEHIND THE TRUTH

The fear of living and even existing was a constant dread with me for a long time. When something as simple as breathing becomes difficult, it's tough to understand your purpose and excel. At eight years old, after my Mother died, I became a victim of molestation.

During her funeral, a family friend who came to mourn with us raped me. When I told my granny about what had happened, she told me to hush. She beckoned for my Auntie to take me to the hospital, and that was it. Heartbroken and grieving my Mom, I felt like I should have died too when my family said I should control the physical pain and never tell a soul. As young as I was, somehow, I knew it wasn't right, and I was internally and emotionally devastated. No one sympathized with me or showed any compassion. It was as if I had done something wrong. I thought at least one would extend a hug or say it would be okay. They pretended it never happened and spoke of it again. For some odd reason, I thought what happened to me was the norm for every Christian home. Throughout my life, I felt so unloved, rejected, and abandoned. In my young mind, covering up sins didn't stop you from being a good Christian. Seem to me it was normal. As I matured, I grew up searching for something to soothe the aching in my heart.

In my search for relief, I was introduced to drugs and alcohol. Those substances were a temporary fix for my deeply rooted wounds. Due to this recklessness, I discovered I was pregnant while training in college. Life became a living hell for me, and my so-called Christian family stopped talking to me because they felt I was an embarrassment. On top of that, my significant other, my baby's daddy, walked out on me when I told him I was pregnant. After that blow, I decided I needed to save myself to save my child. I finally opened my heart and did something for someone else; I quit using drugs and alcohol and decided to get my life together. In my quest for a better life for my baby, I deferred courses in college and went to work. After giving birth to my daughter, three months later, I returned to school. Although I was a single Mom, I was blessed to have help from the ladies at the college's pantry. God hadn't forgotten about me. He sent me some helpers. Against all odds, I completed my college coursework in 2011. I was so excited as the job postings became available; I now had the credentials to apply. I accepted a position believing I was on my way toward a better life when another dilemma knocked at my door. Due to lost paperwork, the examiners said they couldn't give me my certificate because thirteen papers I had written went missing. I ended up working five years without pay.

The challenges I endured within those five years are my most remarkable testimony. This time, I wasn't that eight-year-old little girl who had no control over her life. I was an adult with a child and refused to sleep with anyone, including teachers on campus who decided to punish me by withholding my certificate. Most people would have given up, but I did what the bible said; I turned the other cheek and rewrote those papers over another five years. However, during that time, I started to look at myself differently. I needed answers to why I allowed so many things to happen to me the way they did. I tried to commit suicide at least five times. I tried hanging myself, but the funny thing is that the table I stood on with the rope around my neck broke. After that didn't work, I went to the hardware store and purchased a big jug of pesticide, a poison for killing weeds and insects. I knew this would do it; this poison, when digested, is supposed to kill a human in a few minutes. I drank the entire bottle. Waking up a few hours after being blacked out, I ended up with only horrific stomach pains and still here on earth. GOD came through for me again! But then, a voice of warning and caution spoke to me. "I know the plans I have for you declares the LORD, plans to prosper you and not to harm you; plans to give you hope and a future (Jeremiah 29:11)."

From that day on, I was in search of a higher connection spiritually. When I least expected it, I met Lady Pastor Vera. She was like a breath of fresh air. This woman was an inspiration as she prayed for me and shared God's word as I had never heard before. Lady Vera talked about it and walked in her spiritual gift of ministering to broken and contrite souls. She helped me rekindle my relationship with GOD. Since connecting with her, my life has not been the same. I was sold out for God and took Him at His word that it may form but won't prosper. And that's what's for me; no man could keep it from me.

One day out of the blue, I received a call from the college to pick up my certificate. Those who trashed my papers years ago had been exposed. I'm reminded of God's word, "touch not my anointed, and do my prophet no harm!" He showed up and showed out for me! I love 2nd Timothy 1:7,

For GOD did not give us a spirit of fear;
but of power, love, and a sound mind.

Fear took the best part of my childhood; rejection from friends and family didn't mean rejection from GOD! I lost sight of the love of GOD, and "Truth Be Told," the Holy Spirit was always with me, guiding me. Many people get stuck in addictions and never recover. Others are violated through molestation or raped and end up being prostitutes. But the good word says everything works together for our good. God brought me through it all despite my wrongdoings. In the midst of it all, I have a beautiful twelve-year-old daughter who is like a sister and friend. She filled that void of emptiness and rejection that I carried for so long. I have grown to understand the scripture, "Thou shall love our neighbor as ourselves. (Matthew 22: 37-40). For its only by loving the LORD shall we be saved.

It's by loving oneself; that's how we get to love others truly. The fear of the Lord is the beginning of wisdom. After reading my "Truth," I hope that fear of anything is removed from your spirit and replaced by love. I pray my testimony inspires someone, and they are delivered and set free like I am!

VALERIE & TRENDA DORSEY

TO TELL YOU THE TRUTH
Why Didn't I Just listen...

I remember it like it was yesterday when this nightmare began.
I was a 13-year-old girl with big dreams shattered because she
refused to listen. My mom worked in one of the neighborhood
stores (Joe's Supermarket). I would go to the store every evening
after school to tell my mom I had made it home from school. On
this one particular day in early April of 1980, I was walking in the
back alleyway to my mom's job when I was approached by the most
handsome boy in the neighborhood saying, "hey, Red can you bring
me back an orange soda pop?" of course, I said yes. So, he gave
me a dollar bill and said I could keep the change. My reply was no
thank you because my mom always told my sisters and me if we
accepted anything from boys, they would want something in return.

After I handed him his soda pop, he asked if I wanted to be his
girlfriend. I was flattered but scared at the same time because
I knew better. I shrugged my shoulders with the gesture of
saying, I don't know. He then replied, "yes or no, very strongly."
Apprehensive, I said yes and ran to my friend Ellen to share the
news. As we were gossiping and giggling, I heard him yell my name
and call me back. Once I got up close and personal with him, he
said, "when I call you, whatever you're doing, you better stop and
answer me." I was too young to understand the first signs of abuse.
I was so excited to be dating someone older and handsome too.
With my love for writing, I wrote on any and everything I could
at every chance. I wrote our names on the walls, the front covers
of books, and even on the sidewalk. I just wrote everywhere I
could...Why didn't I listen? My mom saw the writing on the walls
and disciplined me about this boy, not once but repeatedly; still, I
refused to listen. She constantly warned me that he was no good.
I didn't want to hear that; I was in love. Looking back, I was so
rebellious and too grown for my good. I placed myself in difficult
situations because I refused to listen and didn't value my worth. By
the tender age of fifteen, I decided it was time for me to go. I was in
love and wanted to be with him morning, noon, and night. I packed
my bags and moved in with this individual.

After a few weeks of sheer passion, things begin to turn for the worst, but how can that be? He said we're made for each other and that no one or nothing would ever come between our love. Why didn't I listen… This man tried to destroy my very being. I discovered he was extremely jealous and insecure; with characteristics I had never known. He made it clear that I couldn't be around males, including my family members. Any male who looked my way, he would become angry and accuse me of sleeping with them. He attempted to break me down to the least common denominator as he consistently crushed my heart. On one occasion, he took me to Biscayne Blvd and even the Greyhound bus station to prostitute me. Sell my body to strangers! Oh no, I stood my ground this time and refused to oblige. I remember him putting my mouth on a crack pipe; little did I know there wasn't anything in the tube. All of a sudden, the light bulb started to come on. This guy was all up in my head, and speaking of my head, the beatings from him had become so harsh that he would sometimes smash my head into the concrete wall. I can't count the concussions I probably endured. But even worse, the verbal abuse left me emotionally crippled, depressed, and helpless. After so many beatings, my body was immune to physical pain. The straw that broke the camel's back was when he tied me to a chair and threatened to burn his name on my private parts. Why didn't I listen… As time passed and my days continued to darken, I was nineteen years old with a son and was only existing. It should have been a happy time in my life, but it was the opposite.

To top everything off, he was jealous of his son. Whenever he was in a rage, he expressed that his son had taken my love away from him. I know there are questions about why I stayed, but honestly, I still can't answer. Now at twenty-three, with three children in this tunnel of darkness, not knowing or understanding how to escape this feeling of loneliness. I was alone and lost with no family and friends because he had isolated me from everyone. The walls of my apartment were my best friend as I expressed my deepest pains and cried my eyes out for a way out, even contemplating suicide because I felt trapped. Still, I knew I had to be strong for my babies. I felt guilty for the darkness I had brought into their life with no light in sight. As my days grew longer, the abuse worsened, and the control became unbearable. I had to find a way of escape; if not for me, I had to do it for them. Now, my mind is in a state of protection for my innocent babies. One night he was out indulging in drugs and alcohol while I was home relaxing and enjoying a moment of serenity. Suddenly, I heard a knock at the door, and right away, the knots and butterflies in my stomach uprooted a familiar fear inside as I carefully pulled the doorknob. For opening that door, I received the worst beating ever. I was helpless as he spat in my face and used unbelievable objects to abuse me sexually. He tried to kill every piece of my being and then offered that I either return home to my mother's house or be miserable for the duration of my life. It seemed like I had a way out, but returning home with three children to my mother's house wasn't an option, and I didn't take his threats likely. So, I knew only one way out; I had to kill him. One evening, after much thought, I placed my children in the living room while attempting to take their father's life. With hate in my heart, I aimed and pulled the trigger missing his abdominal area by inches. I wanted him to feel what I felt all those years like a dead person walking. I wanted him to die painfully and slowly as I had all those years. But I serve a great God! He heard the cries of my children, which saved their father's life, making me realize that they needed their mother free, not behind a jail cell. "My Truth" is… Why didn't I listen?

GIRL...STAND IN YOUR TRUTH!

Stock photos by Vecteezy.com

BEYONCE KNOWLES CARTER

PATTI MASON

"TRUTH BE TOLD"

He's Dead, I'm Free...

"Ah, you better stop fight! Look out, the police ah come! Look out!" shouted a neighbor as she watched the brawl from her windowless window in the ghetto backstreet of Grays Farm, Antigua. Once all of the dust cleared, and the police left Llewellyn, a troubled, pretty boy who was in the brawl, mother nervously yet firmly instructed him, "you must leave before dem lock you up, go by Goddy she a ga give you some shillings fi go way, go now!" (Antigua Dialect Patwa)

Escorting a female coworker home each night caused jealousy in the town. The pretty boy challenges followed him to Trinidad. Ultimately, he was double-teamed and retaliated, which unfortunately led to a self-defense case. Upon his release in agreement to depart via the judiciary of Trinidad and Tobago, they informed that Loreley was pregnant. He would forever live with the regret of never meeting his unborn child. Bon voyage... Llewellyn set sail for St. Thomas, US Virgin Islands. Upon his settlement, he took no time to make his mark as he embarked on a new clean slate. Once he situated himself into a galvanized efficiency to rent, he worked as a dishwasher.

He eventually utilized his mason, genetic music gifts of entertainment, playing the steel pan, dancing and walking on broken glass bottles to performing gimmicks on his donkeys, earning the name 'Tigo," meaning 'you' in English. Not a native of the tiny paradise island, he was embraced sincerely, eventually meeting the love of his life Dahlia.

Dahlia was the second of six children, born to a humble yet wealthy, hard-working set of parents. Her mother, known by most as Ms. Elena, was a seamstress, originally from Barbados and raised in St. John Virgin Islands, where she met her husband, Dahlia's father Franco of St. John. The young couple moved to St. Thomas and built businesses and the first house on the hills. Dahlia was born sickly yet strong and spent lots of time in her parents' store. Her cousins, along with her cousin like sister Priscilla, whom

Dahlia named her seventh child, a future daughter after, worked hard, not out island hopping on a private yacht as many others did. Dahlia's job included weighing flour, sugar, cornmeal, etc., for store customers. She was petite, fairly light skin with long curly hair, and had slight bowlegs, a Samuel trait.

Llewelyn, now twenty-five years old, met Dahlia at sixteen along her route to school through the garden downtown. It was like love at first sight! With a tan Caribbean complexion, Llewellyn spared no arrogance in pumping his youthful chest out to extenuate his muscular, athletic physique upon his introduction. Dahlia was very dainty, soft-spoken yet affable, With aspirations to become a teacher. Unlike Llewellyn, an alpha male with a British education of a fifth grader equivalent to a US high school graduate, he spoke firmly with a rough Antiguan accent. This hidden inner rage of this sweet damaged Taurus that he is would eventually resurface. In a nutshell, he was an educated hustler from Grays Farm that endured abandonment from a little boy. He often mentioned, "My dad only ever gave me two shillings!...as if it just happened yesterday. "Tigo, you robbing the cradle!" shouted Peter while selling his fruits at the marketplace, simply because Dahlia's appearance was of a child and the known age difference. Not long after dating, Dahlia noticed her health (menstrual) did not show for January. "Tigo, my health did not come for the month!?" Upon Dahlia confiding in her cousin, like sister Priscilla that she is pregnant, she informed Dahlia of a local that does abortions. Ultimately by the time they acquired the funds, it was too late to proceed with an abortion. Tigo knew this was not what he wanted, and apparently, Dahlia's parents would be devastated!

With Dahlia's stomach growing on her perfect hourglass twenty-six-inch waistline, there was only one thing to do, and that was for them to tell her parents. They confessed to Mr. and Mrs. George that marriage was the only way to go. So, they wedded, and Dahlia dropped out of school and dreaded the thought of never becoming a teacher, but the unforeseen was yet to come. The welcoming of baby Iris was short-lived; unfortunately, she never left the hospital and lived only for a little over a month. The family was, and worse, the parents were completely distraught and in disbelief. Baby Iris was laid to rest at a graveside which Dahlia found unbearable to attend. As life and time passed, Dahlia and Llewellyn went on to have six more children traveling the world from Paraguay, Canada, to Puerto Rico, creating a calypso band and limbo gimmicks under the fire that lit up the atmosphere whenever they performed! Settling for five short years in San Juan, Puerto Rico, and buying a home was the beginning of the force division, mental and physical abuse that sat upon the still, petite, dainty, fragile now mother of two. Only a hill's view away when the tides were low seemed impossible when she attempted to escape and return home. When time permitted, and Dahlia could update her parents, she made a run from the pen down of the bull's horn and the fist of steel, only for him to manipulate her to return to another beating, nearly causing her death. Dahlia felt trapped, controlled, and full of regrets, to the point Llewellyn had disconnected her from her friends and family. She had no one to talk to and, at times, sporadically screamed to the top of her lungs, sounding like a wound in the womb. It was an empty howl of pain. Upon the final destination stay in Miami, Florida, Tigo, now known as Mr. Gary, vowed to cease the abuse. Still, it only got worse, along with alcohol abuse, being a gym rat, and promiscuous behavior. Testosterone and his childhood hidden pain did not make anything better. Dahlia, now pregnant with four kids, was a school teacher of the projects. Every morning she would have books, papers, pencils, crayons, a table, and a chair for the children whose mothers allowed them to prepare them for kindergarten.

They'd be sitting on the concrete under the living room window, waiting on Mrs. Martin to start class. Dahlia, a very soft-spoken and sharp wife, mother, and ultimately fulfilling her dreams of being an educator, would attentively and freely teach the children despite feeling trapped. One day when Tigo returned home drunk, pushing his motorcycle up the stairs, the motorcycle fell, and who better than to take his rage out on, as always, Dahlia. He entered the tiny, tidy two-bedroom apartment; after giving and receiving hugs and kisses from the now two teenagers and two preteens, he intentionally picked an argument with Dahlia as she prepared dinner plates for the kids. Tigo would always brag how she was the best mother, with one of her pet peeves of wiping the children's feet off while asleep with a warm rag religiously despite their ages. As Dahlia was preparing the plates, Tigo leaned against the kitchen entrance as he roughly asked Dahlia, "Ya dun tek out da food!?" Guessing Dahlia did not appreciate his tone, she took her time answering him. He then grabbed the pot without considering whether or not she made her plate as he would typically eat right from the pot with his bare hands, like the African tradition once everyone ate. She held onto the pot, screaming to him, "Stop with the foolishness!" One pull and push too hard of the pot landed Dahlia's impregnated, fragile frame on the kitchen floor. That wasn't enough for Tigo as he lunged at her and got a couple of blows in.

Meanwhile, the kids were at the dinner table, and Sandra, the eldest daughter who'd had enough, shouted to the top of her lungs, "Stop it, stop it, that's enough!!" Labeled a tomboy with a Serena Williams build and beauty, the fight ceased after her strong words. It's crazy because the next day, life went on as if nothing had happened. Tigo said, "Dahlia, let's go for a ride," in a gentle tone. To her surprise, she agreed and was somewhat excited to get out of the apartment because she was secluded from all her family and had no friends. They rode to what was known as 'white suburbia,' Carol City. Tigo said, "Pick out a house!" and she did. Bittersweet and short-lived, Dahlia learned that her Papi had suddenly passed away. The check for the estate needed cashing, and only she had the power to do it because she was the beneficiary of his estate. They went on to buy a beautiful four-bedroom two bath home for new beginnings that would only intel the end. Dahlia had her tubes tied after her sixth living child. Boy, oh boy, was Tigo furious when he learned of this. He returned his wife to the hospital, demanding that they untie her tubes, which they did. Two years later, she birthed her seventh and last child. This child was a fair mixture of both personalities. With time and a couple of short years later, Tigo would spend nights out, and the empty howl of entrapment would fill the entire home from the pit of Dahlia's stomach, sometimes traumatizing the kids. She often asked the kids, "Did you see your dad out there?" With all the abuse and him living carefree, they had two twin beds in their room and slept separately.

One night, Tigo backed his work van to the front door, emptied his clothes from the closet, and gathered important documents while aggressively placing them into the van as Dahlia cried and tugged on him, begging him to stay. The youngest, Priscilla, held onto her Mommy's legs while the uncovered bright porch light blared into her youthful eyes. The unexpected howls from Dahlia increased along with her randomly questioning the kids whether or not they'd seen their father. Tigo moved out and on, still controlling the household from another house. As time moved on, the four eldest graduated and moved out. However, when number seven, Priscilla, known as 'the brat,' who was very close to Tigo, now a teenager, came of age and realization, she said to him, "You don't even live here, and you are always telling us what to do!" He fake lunged towards her, who he'd nicknamed Stumpy, as Dahlia put her hand across his chest to block him. As always, when he gets upset, he leaves out the door and speeds off.

Stumpy was the child who was never supposed to be born and had had enough. Number seven orchestrated for the siblings to contribute their equal portion to help buy a new bedroom set for Dahlia. Stumpy emptied her Mom's room of anything that belonged to her father. She replaced the original worn green carpet with a plush pink and painted the walls white. Upon one of Tigo's pop-ups, he said, "Oh, all you tro (throw) all my tings (things)in ah (the) garbage?" Stumpy rolled her eyes sarcastically, ignored him, and continued with the improvements. With the rehab of the house, Dahlia begins to see her self-worth. She felt a sense of pride, appreciativeness, and confidence and even began keeping her bedroom door closed. She would go on to babysit her grandkids, watching the morning news and talk shows while sitting on the floor, her comfy place. Tigo's visits became increasingly rare as his vision began to leave him from glaucoma. They were narrowed down to once a week via his now-wife escorting him from Overtown Miami to Carol City on Sundays. He enjoyed bringing the grandchildren cheeseburgers and fries from McDonald's.

Eventually, Stumpy begins visiting him with her two kids, naming her son after Llewellyn for her father's love, despite the bright light from the memorable night darkening her view on what she'd tolerate from men. As Tigo's health diminished, he would start making remorseful confessions to his adult children while on his death bed, saying, "I mistreated your Mommy." Stumpy replied, "Daddy, it's ok." "No, really, really bad!" Her response to him, with a calm reassurance tone, was, "Daddy, WE forgive you!" He sighed deeply, closed his eyes, and turned his head away. His days were short, and he had hospital stays often. Once his organs began to shut down, all nine of his children and two "wives" were present at the bedside, except for Stumpy, who chose not to keep that as a final vision. Later, the "great" Tigo closed his eyes and transitioned from this earthly realm. The funeral service was held at a Catholic Cathedral in Overtown. One of Tigo's oldest friends, which he didn't keep many because of his shenanigans, played the steel pan beautifully during the service. It was as if you could feel Tigo's Spirit with every ping from the steel pan. After everyone made their way to their vehicles to go to the burial grounds, "Truth be Told," his first love, Dahlia quietly made her way back into the cathedral to kiss the only love of her life goodbye.

YOUR DEEPEST THOUGHTS

Which "Truth" can you relate to?

_____

_____

_____

_____

_____

What will you do now that you've faced the Truth?

_____

_____

_____

_____

_____

What plan of action will you develop to move forward as you walk in your Truth?

_____

_____

_____

_____

_____

_____

_____

_____

_____

CHAUNQUAVIA MANUEL

MOMENT OF TRUTH

Oh, what a life I've lived! So much trauma, strife, abuse, sadness, and pain during my childhood. "Truth be Told," I chose to talk about it because it still affects me and has caused me to suffer from significant depression throughout my life. It all began in 2007 after my great-grandmother's death. She was more than my protector and greatest supporter; she was my friend. When it was all said and done, she was my life!

Shortly after her death, I had to go live with my mom, where I was so lost and lonely. I believe my mom loved me, but just not as my great-grandmother did. A few months after my great-grandmother's death, one rainy night at my aunt's house, my sleep was suddenly disturbed as I slept peacefully. My male older cousin woke me up and told me to lie on the floor. I still remember everything vividly, as if it was yesterday. My cousin aggressively tried to penetrate me in my private area as I lay on the floor obediently, but it wouldn't fit... I was such a young child, a minor; how could he! I gave it my all as I tried to push him off me with all my might. My body was trembling, and I was in deep fear. Like a running faucet, tears ran down my face. I was so afraid to scream as he tried his best to push it, force it, and break me open as if he was an electric drill trying to screw a nail into a wall! Remind you, I was only like seven years old, and I firmly believe he was seventeen with a body like a grown man. After that night, the depression started all over again. My mind and spirit went to a very dark place. I didn't know who to trust. The sad part about that molestation is that he acted as if it never happened. Here I am, unhappy, lonely, in pain, disconnected, depressed on the verge of suicide. I lived in that place alone, never telling anyone because I didn't know how.

Why didn't I tell my mom? Why didn't I tell my teacher? Why, why, why? Well, my mom wasn't the motherly type to keep your secrets, and I didn't tell my teacher because I didn't trust her either.

I decided only to trust the voices in my head... like I did everything else. I was in a broken home with a broken heart for years. Although the house was full of other siblings, we each had our problems and issues. My oldest brother abused my oldest sister physically as if she was a man on the streets.

Although she was young, she had to be an adult cooking for me and all six of my brothers and sisters at the tender age of fourteen. I watched her, so over-whelmed, so used and unhappy too. Like all of us, her going to school was an option.

I chose to go to that place of learning, but I stayed to myself. Many kids and adults thought I was crazy because I was a loner, and I still am.

Although I didn't care about school, it was a part-time escape and gave me peace from my depression at home. But, as soon as I returned, the shenanigans would start again. On one occasion, that older brother slapped my baby brother, and when I asked him why he did it, he ran after me attempting to hit me too. I was a fast runner, so I took off for the backyard, hiding under this wood door-shaped board. I remember seeing a transparent object peeping through the dirt, glistening in the dry, brownish, unkept grass. I reached down, picked up the small piece of glass, and for some odd reason, started to rub it across my left wrist. That's when it all began; I was cutting myself and eventually became what's known as a cutter. At that time, I didn't know how to deal with pain; blades and knives were my only comfort option. I needed to feel something. It made me think, feel, and have a sense of winning. It was my secret... As I share this "Truth," I want you to know that if I had a chance to return to my childhood, I wouldn't. Although I have so many truths, I want to share this one because I believe someone reading this needs to know that God will, if you ask Him, deliver you as He did me. I remember the night I walked home alone, leaving the park; a man asked me if I wanted a ride home because it was dark.

He told me he was afraid for me to be out by myself at night and that the area wasn't safe, especially for young girls like me. Being young, vulnerable, and naive, he tricked me into trusting him. Like a gentleman, he got out and pulled the knob on the door, opening the door for me. Oh wow, I thought, no one has ever done that for me. As I settled in and pointed toward my street address, the man kept driving as I looked at the neighborhood elementary school. I became petrified as I told him to stop and let me out. He started talking the grownup sweet talk to me and, with his free hand, began rubbing parts of my body with his free hand. As I stared at the front windshield in bewilderment, this sounds crazy, but it felt good. I was still scared, but his touch gave me a warmth I had never felt. When he saw me settle down, he pulled the truck over as I sat frozen in the passenger seat, climbing over and spreading my legs as my cousin did years ago. That night, I was robbed again of my God-given purity, but this time by a stranger. I broke...

I finally realized the terror I'd been through as a child. The light bulb came on as I faced my why, to why I've been through so much. My God, as I share my "Truth, did it take all of that to make me firm in my stance and be the phenomenal woman I am today? God, I surrender to selflessness instead of selfishness... I am sharing my testimony with the world. Although it hurt... Although I cut myself to release the pain. Although molested, verbally and physically abused, raped, and everything else, you saved me and set me free from childhood abuse. I gave myself to God and forgave those who hurt me wholeheartedly. It took me a while to get here, but I love them because if they had not done to me what they did, I wouldn't be the powerfully anointed woman I am today. I pray that whoever reads this "Truth," my testimony, will help them overcome childhood hurt, be healed from the burden, bitterness, and brokenness, and like me, finally be set free. God bless you all!

VERA OFORI AKOMAH

"TRUTH TO POWER!"
"It's More Than An Emotion..."

A few days after, I returned from missions (soul-winning) at a town in the Volta region of Ghana; while scrolling through Facebook, I saw that I had over five hundred (500) friend requests on my list. As I scrolled through the names, I chose a few and accepted this gentleman who seemed quite unique. We started chatting on Messenger, and eventually, we met in person. His becoming a friend was not difficult because we attend the same church. "Truth be Told," when we first met in church, he was exactly how I described the kind of man I wanted to be married to in my heart. Our age difference didn't matter; his stature, career aspirations, etc., were all aligned with what I needed in my life. After a few months of friendship, he proposed to me, and I answered positively because I had been praying and waiting for that moment. My relationship with him started on a good note. We shared incredible moments in church and outside church activities, young adults' meetings, missions to rural communities, dates, etc. As time went on, we began to face reality. The authentic self began to show, and it was alarming.

The insults at the slightest provocation were difficult to believe. It was nothing that any woman would like to experience, especially when you knew your worth. I cried, prayed, and pleaded with the Lord to deliver me from that relationship. Surprisingly, it lasted for about two years.

Let me save the details for another day. I discovered, and now I can share, that when you enter a relationship, do not turn deaf ears and a blind eye to negative signs: disrespect, hostility, controlling behaviors, lack of support, and the rest. They are the same things you will experience in marriage if not deterred. Love is a personal decision. It means being committed to someone with the sole purpose of bringing the best in and out of them without inducing them to sin against God, themselves, or others. Love should not be forced on you. When it becomes unbearable, seek help, speak out, or leave. Only you have the keys to your closet. So, be very careful about who you release them to. This was my first attempt at a relationship; so many infidelities were on my side too. The shortcomings I couldn't handle, so I became vulnerable and helpless. I handled the situation according to my level of knowledge. At a point, I blamed myself and other reasons for his awkward actions and inactions; nevertheless, I realized at the eleventh hour that a relationship is "More than an Emotion." I call it the eleventh hour because we were left with a few months to our wedding day. How could I let this relationship go after plans had been made? **"Truth be Told,"** I had no other choice. If I didn't learn anything else, I now know that a relationship is the decision of two or more people to seek the welfare of each other. It should be reciprocal and not lopsided. The connection is more than butterflies in the stomach; a love shared in a relationship is beyond emotions or mere affection. Going on outings, shopping, traveling worldwide, dinner parties, etc. Is it just the icing in a relationship? How about the substance, the cake? What do you feel for a man alone who cannot sustain the relationship? At first, I thought I knew a lot about the subject since most of my friends were adults and had jumped from one relationship to the other. Many shared their ins and outs with me; I even counseled some, though I had no experience.

I'm not an expert, but I know that a relationship is the foundation of marriage, and to enjoy a good marriage, you must build a good foundation. "If the foundations are destroyed, what can the righteous do?" Proverbs 11:13. Take this stage of your life seriously whether you are a woman or advanced in age. Age should never propel you to make a hasty decision. Friends and family should not compel you to rush into it. Be the captain of your ship and take charge of its happenings so you can control every responsibility that comes with it. Please permit me to share four things I discovered the hard way that transformed my life for good.

First, define what you are and stay focused: the defining moment is a crucial thing that you don't have to overlook. You have to reach a level where you can realize, know and accept yourself from your inner self to your outward look. You have no co-equal because your kind has never existed before. Being your best version and realizing, knowing, and accepting yourself attract people who will love, respect, and appreciate your energy. Add even more value to yourself by learning more and getting to know yourself better; your temperament, default style of interaction, strengths and weaknesses, likes and dislikes, and your love language and fight language. Do you have what you are looking for in a partner?

Secondly, don't ignore the God factor: let not the relationship be for only the two of you but make Christ Jesus the center of it. One of my favorite scripture is Proverbs 3:5-6 " Trust in the LORD with all your heart and lean not to your understanding. In all your ways, acknowledge him, and he shall direct your paths." This scripture reminds us that God is interested in our affairs. He wants to be with you through it all; share the sorrowful and joyful moments, failing and winning with you. Don't leave Him behind. Let him be in the known and seek to know God's will concerning your relationship or marriage. He wishes you to prosper and be in good health (3 John 1:2). Tell Him, and cry on Him when necessary. He loves you!

Third, make each other a priority: there is nothing like "am I your size?" in a relationship. The moment both parties agree to reciprocally better the life of each other, you also settle on one neutral level. Don't rate yourself above anyone. Be committed to each other, and don't be selfish. When there is no kindness, selfishness fills the gap. Be interested in your partner's progress and encourage them to be their best self.

Lastly, live within your right: no matter the height you reach in life as a woman, give your partner the honor as the head of the family. The fundamental love language of every man is respect and not food. Avoid comparing him to your ex or other men. Most marriages and homes are breaking down because some women want to live like their husbands even in their presence. There is no laid down procedure or 101 ways to marry. Define your own rules and create your theory for the relationship or marriage. You must have trust, respect, submission, tolerance, forgiveness, compatibility, enhanced communication, and intimacy; these traits will keep the relationship healthy. Relax and do not rush into it, or else you will rush out. Your marriage will blossom! Be blessed!

FEEL YOUR TRUTH!

GLORIA ESTEFAN

PANITRA JACKSON

AIN'T IT THE TRUTH?!!!

Some things in life leave us completely broken, devasted, and scarred for a lifetime. Often these life events are beyond our control, yet the hurt and scorn are everlasting. My devastation nearly sent me off the deep end. In 2015, I was trying to rebound from the death of a previous lover, who was so significant to my life that I could not explain it in mere words. However, the end of this lover's life was so unexpected. His committing suicide would take me entirely by shock. I had known of a federal indictment that involved a wiretap out of Saint Petersburg, Florida. After reading the lengthy charge, I understood why the FEDs were called the Alphabet boys. I can remember it just like it was yesterday. It was early September. It was screeching hot, one of the hottest days that year. The sweat had trickled down my chest effortlessly.

It was sweltering, like the day Dr. King preached about. It was so hot that the heat swept through my shoes, my toes, and every bone in my body. Before this date, there had been signs of mental illness and stress.

There had been the constant request for him to come live with me; of course, the request was denied because my house was already full. On this day, I was at work and received a call from my Godbrother and my ex's best friend. He confided in me that he was afraid. He said he could not return to prison again. He had already done a seven-year stint in Killeen, Texas, for trafficking drugs through the United States Postal system. He had violated his probation and did another ten months for being in the company of a known felon. He was stern about not ever doing another day. He asked if anyone had called me. I replied to him, no. I wondered why I was being asked this question because he had repeated himself about five to six times. And then he hit me with it. My ex-lover Jonathan drove to a location, gave his girlfriend thirty thousand dollars, and after she entered the building, he blew his brains out. I was crushed mentally, fainted, and could no longer perform. I had to leave work. I had to break this news to my 15-year-old son, whom Jonathan had taken care of since he was four. It was almost like we were in complete shock, without closure. There were so many rumors whirling around. They said Jonathan was an informant and working with the FEDs. About eight people had already been indicted in connection to the wiretap. The funeral was at an undisclosed location, compliments of his "Hating Azz" ex. (The Predator, because her teeth seemed to stick out and retract, back into her mouth, like one). For months, my entire family, friends, acquaintances, and enemies tried to make sense of it, but we couldn't. There was a void, an emptiness that consumed me. This man was everything to me, not because he was once my lover, but because he was most of my trusted friends.

If my back was against the wall, he was always superman to the rescue, and I, Lois Lane, to him. I could not move on from this point; it was as if I was stuck. Only one person could comfort me during this time, and he and I had not spoken for months.

He was my father, Jerry Jackson. My father and I had not spoken for some time.

I believe it had something to do with the fact that he had cursed me out at the hospital because I had accused him of relapsing and using heroin. Of all my father's children, I was a child that he disclaimed. Why? I believe it has something to do with my mother and her sexuality. I was a child born to a young woman at the age of seventeen who, probably at that age, was confused about her sexuality. She was the youngest of three daughters, and her sisters were twenty and twenty-two years older than she was. My grandmother Florence Bivins-Woods was stern and strict with my mother. My grandmother was born in 1919 in rural Wildwood, Florida. She was stuck in her ways and unable to change or alter her way of thinking. It was what it was, and it is what it is, my grandmother would say. Around November, my father came to me, and with the most shocking thing, he apologized for how he treated me, talked to me, and most of all, for not being there when Jonathan died. My dad said he knew I was devastated, but his stubbornness stopped him from coming to me during my time of need, yet he came to me in his. My father had been diagnosed with prostate cancer.

Of all nine of his children, I think that he knows that I was the one child who was always there for him through his crack addiction, his heroin addiction, through him being a complete jackass, but this was the point at which he needed me to be there for him again.

I cried and wailed in my father's arms as I expressed how broken my heart was for losing my friend, who was so much more to my entire family and me. My father had confessed to me that he had prostate cancer. It was the second time my father had faced some form of cancer. He had already had polyps removed from his rectum. Although our relationship was tumultuous, I became very involved in my father's medical affairs taking him to doctor's appointments and making sure he took his medication. His robotic-assisted prostate surgery was a success at the University of Miami hospital. He even babysat my newborn baby at times.

I came home one day, and my neighbor called me and said something was wrong with my father: he thought my father was high. He had told me they had to stop my father from walking in front of a bus and that he felt he had tried to commit suicide. I was looking forward to more years with my dad. My father has been living with me since his surgery because he needed my son and me to care for him, which is what we did. We did our best to take care of him. My father had always had his apartment not too far from where I lived.

I explained to him father, "I have children, and you cannot get high at my house in front of my kids. If you want to get high, then you can go home to your house."

You don't have your father getting high around your children in your place. I thought that at that time, I was making the correct choice. It was the right thing to do. So, I sent my father home. I sent him on his way. I remember passing by his house, and my eldest son told me, "Mommy, we should go stop and see about granddad. I replied I'm kind of angry with granddad. I think that he needs to breathe. I wish I had listened to my son. I got a phone call from my son's father, who told me that someone had called him and said they had not seen Jerry in a couple of days and that a foul odor was coming from his house. I had gotten this call before, so I wasn't alarmed. My boyfriend has a Tom, and I went to go and see my father. My father was so skeptical about people and things that he had a chain lock that went through his bar gate, door, and window to keep people out. When we got there, the smell of death was in the air. There were flies around his door, and I felt my father was dead inside his house. We left to get bolt cutters so we could cut through for locks. It took a while, but we were successful. I said he was dead as I walked up the stairs and down the hallway. The neighbor told me that you are very calm. I said what is it that you can do? What could I do? He's already dead. I know my father was dead. When I entered my father's house, I heard his air conditioner on, and when I opened the door to his room, the flies came out. My father was kneeling. His shirt had burst open; bodily fluids had seeped from his body, but maggots were everywhere. My father died in the house from a fentanyl overdose two days. I was devastated. She completely overwhelmed me with the pain, the grief, the hurt, the guilt, the anger.

My father was put away very well, considering his body could not be viewed because he was so decomposed. The Fire Rescue had refused to remove his body from the house. His bodily fluids had seeped from his body. I called a friend at the Funeral Home, and they came and got my father's body. My two brothers and I waited four hours until 4:00 am. They broke my father's bones to get him inside the body bag. My brothers had to assist the funeral assistant in carrying their dead father down three flights of stairs. Seeing this caused my breakdown. I was numb at my dad's wake, viewing, and funeral. I wish I could have a do-over with him. Why didn't I listen to my son? I wanted so many different things that I could not take back. I could not function in any capacity, which caused me to stay off work for two weeks. Although I was in this state, my principal insisted that I did not need a break and needed to return to work. She was not thinking of me at all. Her only concern was the students and their reading scores. Despite what I felt, I returned to work, but not much of anything got done. I managed to teach my students without grading papers or writing lesson plans. My students managed to do very well on the Florida State Assessment while their teacher fell to pieces. I decided to see a therapist, was diagnosed with depression and adult ADD and was prescribed Buitron, Adderall, and Seroquel.

I don't think anyone who has not lost a parent can't understand the loss that one feels after losing a parent. No one could ever imagine how manically depressed I was after finding my father there the way I saw him. I wish I could take it back every day, but I can't. I move forward in life, trying to make amends with my soul for not paying attention to my daddy.

BONITA "PEACHES" DAVIS

NOTHIN' BUT THE TRUTH

September 15, 1993 is the day I hate to remember. A lifetime to you, but it's as if it was yesterday to me. On this day, a part of my soul left, and my heart was crushed into a million pieces. As I once knew it, my life would never be the same.

Me and TJ, my youngest son, were outside on the side of the house, just standing around, when he said Mama, Carleton is leaving on someone's bike. I looked around, and my oldest son was waving at me. Earlier, he had told me he wanted to go over to the projects because he had bought a pager from someone, and they still hadn't given it to him. I told him, I moved you guys away from there so you would be safer. He responded, but all my friends are there. As he turned the corner, I yelled, come back before dark! He replied with his contagious dimpled smile, "okay," not knowing it would be our last earthly goodbye. TJ and I went back inside the house to watch television with my other kids, not knowing my world would come crashing down in a few hours. The doorbell, accompanied by a fierce pounding on the door, startled me. I thought it was Carleton and his friends playing around; as I flung the door open, two of his friends stood crying and screaming his name. They yelled it's Carleton, Ma'am; he got hit! What are you talking about, child? Hit where? He got hit by a car on the bridge around the corner; Carleton said to come and get you! I think I was in shock as if I had an out-of-body experience.

As I stood there, my body and mind screaming simultaneously, I pleaded with God, "please, not my son." I ran to the car with the boys and my daughter Marie begging to go to her brother. But my youngest was there and couldn't be left alone. So, I left Marie behind to care for them. The Baseline bridge was just around the corner, but it seemed like it was taking an eternity to get there. When I pulled up, I left the car running with the door open as I jumped out and ran up that long bridge. I had to get to him to let him know; Mommy's here, baby. As I approached the scene, I yelled, is he okay? Is he alive? I wanted them to say yes, he's just bruised. All I could see was the massive crowd on the bridge and my son lying in the middle of the street, covered with a black blanket. My legs gave out, and I fell to the ground beside my baby. Carleton, are you okay? Can you hear me, baby? When he slowly lifted his hand for me, I saw it was bloody and bruised. I looked at my child lying there. I was unable to help nor save him. My mind drifted back to when he once wrote a story for school saying, I love my Mommy; she's always there to help me. My heart ached as I realized I couldn't do what he said in that story. I felt like the most horrible person in the world. I felt helpless. He tried desperately to open his eyes as I spoke, "Mommy's here, son. Can you hear me?" He tried to nod yes, as I searched desperately for the ambulance that still hadn't arrived. I screamed to the top of my lungs, "Please, God! Please, somebody, help him! My head and eyes shifted as I noticed across the street my son mangled bicycle. I turned back quickly as I looked down and saw my son's feet with no shoes. What the Hell! Did someone take them off him? Then I looked and noticed that his socks and shirt were missing too. I could hear my Grandmother's still voice; if one shoe is gone, you're not going anywhere, but if both shoes are gone, you won't need them because you will be getting a new pair in heaven. My heart hurt so bad. I asked my dear child, Carleton, are you leaving me? My voice was trembling so severely from crying. He nodded yes, and I said no, you don't know what you're saying. As I lifted his face to the side, I saw the deep opening in his face. I screamed, God, please, please don't take my child.

Finally, I heard the loud sirens of the ambulance; I stood there screaming moans from where the most unimaginable pain must reside. Standing there, a young girl approached me, crying. I'm so sorry she said, I tried to get to him, but as I was running to him, the other car ran him over and kept going. I almost fainted; what other car hit my son? Do you mean to tell me two cars hit Carleton? Why, oh God, why did she have to say this to me? My spirit cried out, and the pain was too much to bear.

They lifted my son battered body into the ambulance, I tried to climb in, but they kept pushing me away. I'm his Mother, please, he needs me! Please, I beg of you, but they told me they had to work on him. He's critical; follow the ambulance, Ma'am. No one understood that I needed to get in there to hold him and let him know he wasn't alone. I ran back to the car and begged someone to please go and get my children and bring them to the hospital. I pulled up to the hospital and ran inside, looking for my child. All I saw was the gurney holding my son, rushing quickly past my children and me. Marie, my oldest, TJ, my daughter Kombey and Torie waited in that waiting room for what seemed forever. Marie and I couldn't stop vomiting. They rushed us to the bathroom because it was going everywhere. Looking back, I'm sure it was from shock. I could hear my children's cries as they pleaded with God too.

It was about four hours later when the Doctor walked out. I remember the cleanliness of his uniform. It was as if he hadn't operated on my son at all. My heart stood still as I thought, "please, just say he's going to be okay." Unemotional, he just stood there and said that he was gone. What do you mean he's gone? Gone where? Please, what do you mean? God, you would not take my son, the one who prayed every night until he would fall asleep on his knees. Not the child who begged to go to church, who read his bible every night before he went to sleep. The Doctor was still standing there, I could hear him talking, but I wasn't there. I remember him saying that Carleton's spleen was ruptured, and they couldn't stop the bleeding.

All I felt was my feet lifting and my body moving; I ran down the long hall, searching for the room holding my son. I finally found my baby. The space was empty, and there lay my son's lifeless body. I reached down and pressed his semi-warm body to mine. I held onto him as I whispered, baby, please wake up for Mommy. My oldest child Marie entered the room and stood next to me screaming. Those screams pierced my soul. My son TJ ran out of the hospital, crying that his big brother was gone. I held Carleton's body until they finally pulled me away.

That night for me, for my children, was the coldest, most horrible night of our lives. I gave up on God that night, never wanting to pray again. I also gave up on life. Living with such a terrible loss was unbearable. My life spun out of control, and I had a nervous/mental breakdown. I couldn't be there for my kids because the woman I knew had left with my son that night.

71

As the years have passed, I think about my poor children, losing their brother and their Mom mentally gone simultaneously. As I write these last words, I have survived losing my son; they have too, but the loss has taken an enormous toll on us. I now pray for mothers everywhere who have endured the loss of a child. You never get over it but learn to live with the pain. You have to find a way to go on for the love of your children and loved ones that are still with you.

YOUR DEEPEST THOUGHTS

Which "Truth" can you relate to?

_____

_____

_____

_____

_____

What will you do now that you've faced the Truth?

_____

_____

_____

_____

What plan of action will you develop to move forward as you walk
in your Truth?

_____

_____

_____

_____

_____

_____

_____

_____

LAQUISHA WILLIAMS

GOD HONEST TRUTH

"Crossroads - a point at which a crucial decision must be made that will have far-reaching consequences."

I suspect that we all have come to crossroads in our lives. It may have been a decision to marry, have children, leave your nine to five, and become an entrepreneur or not. To stay comfortable or pull the plug on a loved one or not. Stay in a relationship that's taking away from you or adding to your life or not. Should I go left or right? Do I go straight or stay on the same path? Whatever it may be, you had to decide, not knowing the outcome, results, or consequences. All you know is that you must make a decision and make a decision fast! So, when you have arrived at a crossroads in life, what is one to do? Crossroads are not limited to consequences. They come in all shapes and sizes. Another definition of crossroads is a "place where change happens." Each person reading this book has reached a point on whether to love or not love the person they see in the mirror. Which, at times, can be our greatest challenge. I've said it often that it doesn't matter what has happened to you, but how you respond to what has happened to you. Whatever your decision or response may be, that will determine your life's direction. Pause for a moment: Are you facing a crossroads?

What choices will you make that determine how you author your own life? Harley Davidson says, "When writing your life story, don't let anyone else hold the pen." You must decide that at the end of your chapter, there should be lessons and life experiences to help you become a trailblazer and world-class woman. You should not still be on chapter one, stuck in your story, stuck in what someone did to you, stuck in unforgiveness when you should be on chapter forty-two, where you are receiving double for your trouble. At this point, you should be in a place where lives have changed. Why? It's because of a decision you've made at the crossroad.

Crossroads are not necessarily "Good" or "Bad," but what we do can cause a lasting effect on our lives for the good or the bad. For instance, staying in a relationship with someone who continues to abuse and take advantage of you may compromise your beliefs and morals to "fit in" a particular group or clique. Whatever decision you make can cause a significant change in your life because change is inevitable. Many people have gotten so used to inadequate or good treatment that when faced with a challenge disguised as a crossroad, they do not know what to do. Remember, it's not merely about what has happened to you but how you handle the change. Crossroads have caused me to become VERY uncomfortable, but trust me, the results are endless. Continue on this journey with me...

Many of you have heard motivational speakers, business coaches, and religious leaders say, "Your comfort zone is your danger zone." Let that sink in... For me, I was trying to do things undercover. I was trying to do something that would be easy and would not challenge me to become my best self. I almost diminished the quality and actual substance of who God created me to be because of my crossroad. I always knew I would be great, but I was floating in the sea of average, mediocrity, people pleasing, fear, low self-esteem, self-sabotage, and doubt. I know some of you were swimming with me too!! We never accomplish as much as we'd like when we only do the things that don't test us, stretch us, challenge us, or generally make us feel out of our "element." When we go beyond our regular routines, sweet spots, and "no-brainer" abilities, we get ahead and achieve things beyond the norm. When you continue to do something, knowing what the outcome will be, your life will be BORING!! Sometimes when you make the hard decisions, you have better results. You end up being a better person. You may ask, why is that Laquisha? It's because everything you've been through was to bring you to where you are right now. You are who you are today from your choices at the crossroads. Crossroads will take you out of your comfort zone and make you work for it, which means you must keep digging.

Growing up, when we didn't do something right at home, my mom would say, if you don't succeed at first, try and try again. Although the crossroad may be scary, sometimes making a difficult decision causes you to see who you are and what you are. At the end of it all, you must realize that you were born for your assignment....you must "Trust the Process." Everything happens for a reason, and many times we are the main reason some things happen. We don't understand how much power we have and how strong we are until we decide at a crossroads. I dare you to take one step in the direction you want to go. Yes, the road may look different, the people may speak a different language, the people may not look like you, you may be leaving behind your family, and the land may be unfamiliar....but again, you must "Trust the Process." When facing a crossroads, you will have to choose to determine how you will author your life. One thing to remember is that, although change is often uncomfortable, it is not "bad" or "good " by definition. But what we choose to do during these times can determine our character, who we will eventually be, and what legacy we will leave. At the crossroad, there are a lot of things that may be going through our minds. I want to make the step. I don't want to make a step. I want to love my perfect imperfections; I don't want to love my flaws. It was always a back-and-forth for me. At the crossroad of not loving who I was and what I saw in the mirror. I noticed that I was different... It took me a while to realize that what set me apart was not a burden, but it's what makes me great.

As you read my "Truth," I don't want you to feel sorry or have pity for me, but to hear my struggle and how I had to decide at the crossroad. Many women and men take too much energy and time trying to see how they can blend in. You don't ever want to be average. Like I said earlier, being normal is boring. Maya Angelou said, "when you know better, you do better." After all, why be ordinary when you can be exceptional?! When something "fits in," it is too easy to blend in, to go completely unnoticed. But when something stands out, you cannot help but notice it. You cannot help but have your attention drawn to it. Now, I am not talking about standing out in your physical appearance – I am talking about standing out in your character. I am talking about being proud of where you came from. I am talking about being happy with the family you were born in. I am talking about standing out by going the extra mile, being extra kind and compassionate toward others, by living a life of integrity. In today's world, those qualities will definitely make you a person who stands out. Every day we have the choice to stand out. Every day we have the option to focus on being fabulous to go beyond the average or the typical. We have the choice to be exceptional. I can hear my parents saying it now, why follow the crowd when you can be leading it? Why shoot for the ordinary when you can be spectacular? Although it had been a struggle for many years because the scenery and the people sounded different, I had to dig deep and be confident with the sound coming from my mouth. After all, I would not be myself if I lost a part of my being amazing. It confused me when I heard people who came from where I came from sound different from me. They lost their accent and who they were, but although I tried, I never lost mine, and now I stand out. Be confident to stand up for what is right, even when you are the only one doing it. Don't lower your standards to fit in with the crowd. Instead, let your example be what lifts others around you to raise their standards to yours. This may be something you have to face at the crossroad, blending in with the "majority." I assume if you're reading my chapter, you must be a leader, and if you are a leader, you lead by example.

So, as I end my chapter and stand in my "Truth," here is my crossroad... I was considered ghetto or hood in my teenage years because of my name, Laquisha. But now, I'm an adult, not because of what I said or did but because of my name. While working, when I would introduce myself, my students would say, "you've got a ghetto name." I also remembered a friend of my cousin saying, what are you doing with that "hood" name? They left me speechless. Society has contaminated us so much that just because a few people did something, that negative assumption would judge everyone.

Even in the life of reality TV, you see a lot of women either using a shorter version of their name or using a middle name because they are ashamed of their names. It seems as though no matter how high you get in life, people are always trying to be something they're not. I was like those women too on reality TV. I thought of ways to change my name so people could not look at me a certain way. This thought carried on even in dating. I introduced myself to this guy I dated for a short time as Laquisha, but later that week, when we spoke on the phone, he told me, now tell me, what's your real name? I'm like, that is my real name. He said the only Laquisha he knows live in the hood, with at least six kids, purple hair, and many tattoos. I didn't know how to respond because he was cute, and I was shocked. I was unfamiliar with the things he listed, but I replied that I have none of the above and that he should not judge people because it can be very offensive. He made me think of things I had never done before. I even went to the courthouse to find out how to legally change the name I'd had for twenty-one years. I remember asking my mother why she gave me that name. She was always at the crossroads providing me with great advice. She said my name was given to me in love just like I was made in love. This crossroad was one with many lessons to learn. I've encountered other adults telling me that once I introduced myself, the first thing they would say was, you don't look like a Laquisha. Hmmm…, so now Laquisha has a "look." The journey at the crossroad continues.

I remembered dating my first love, with whom I was head over heels, and after four years, he found someone else. Someone lighter and smaller than I was. I remember crying to him, pleading and begging him to take me back. I begin asking him questions like, is it because I'm dark? Is it my accent? Is it my weight? Although it happened many years ago, I remembered it like it was yesterday. He held me by both hands and said,

"Listen to you. Do you hear what you're saying?" He went on to say, "You deserve someone better."

Due to where I was at my crossroad, I was not willing to accept that. I just wanted to change my identity so he could be with me. I said to myself; there's something you can do. Seeing so many commercials for cosmetic surgery, I said this could be something I could do. Now, keep in mind that we are not together anymore. I was lonely and frustrated. I went and had a consultation on getting some procedures done. I got the date for my surgery, made my payment, and was ready to have a beach body to get my boyfriend back. I just wanted him to have an attraction for me. I wanted him to want me back as I wanted him. The date came for the surgery, and I remembered being awakened by the doctor. Because I was still under medication, I was going in and out. My friend, who I trusted to take care of me after the surgery, was there with me. I feel my stomach, no cuts, trying to understand what's happening. The doctor said the procedure had to be on hold because I didn't have medical clearance. Medical clearance? I was so upset because I would not be able to show my ex-boyfriend my "New body." My mission of being transformed didn't happen as I wanted it. Many people are on missions to do things for others, for someone else's approval or even validation. Do you know one person who is currently doing that? Or is the person you?

My crossroad of self-discovery and self-love has been rough. Writing this chapter has brought back many memories I wanted to ignore and forget. I had all these big dreams, but because I was not ready to accept who I was and all that came with me, it left me stagnant. It left me stuck at the crossroad of accepting myself. Stagnation is the enemy of progress, but sometimes, it's easy to get caught up in everything we want to change about ourselves and forget all the beautiful things we already have going! I know it's hard for women to accept a compliment, or when someone says something good about you, we would always go with what's wrong with us. What I've had to do was say kind words about me, from me. If you're not doing so, start today! Start talking to yourself. Encourage yourself. Stop waiting at the crossroad for somebody to come by and tell you how fabulous you are.

I know for some people, it's much, much easier said than done. There was a time when I would've found it difficult to name three things I liked, let alone loved, about myself. Happily, today I could move from that crossroad and share my story with others. After sharing my story with others, I received many messages from people who struggle to let go of their negative self-perception and fall in love with themselves and their life. To all you lovely people out there, I have two big things to say: Self-love takes time. It's a process, a never-ending journey. Don't be discouraged if you don't fall head-over-heels in love with yourself as soon as you start. Self-love is made of lots of little actions, like saying good things to yourself. Every little step you take towards loving yourself will help you love yourself more. Falling in love with yourself can seem pretty daunting when you are at a crossroads alone. Finding answers at the crossroads will always have you in motion. You must do something, and it doesn't have to be something big, but you must commit to the process: even though you may feel like a weirdo.

If you do some of these things initially, I promise that something magical will happen if you stick to it. So, I say to you, no matter how you look, how you may sound, no matter what your name is, that whatever others say about you, how others feel about you, DOES NOT MATTER. You must be able to come to your crossroad and decide that no one will determine the outcome of your life and accept yourself. The only person that can get the desired results you want would be you. Make the decision not to sit at the crossroad. Yes, I know it hurts; you feel like you must get revenge and want to blend in so that it can be easier, but that's not who you are. There is greatness within you that's waiting to come out. There's greatness within you that is lying dormant that needs to be activated. You may be at a crossroads, and your battery has died. You may feel that everyone is passing you by, and no one is stopping to see if you need something; no one is asking how they can assist you. You can look at this in two ways; maybe some people are waiting for you to make a move, saying, "I shouldn't want it more than her." She wants to live beneath her potential. But know, you were not called to be mediocre; you were called to be great! You are called to the nations!

You have a chapter that's yet to be written. What legacy are you willing to leave behind? You have to be proud of your story and not look at it as a disappointment, but look at what you've been through as life lessons. Some learn faster than others but stay in your lane. Do not try to go ahead of your story, and don't look at the whole staircase. Decide to take one step at a time and be activated! Just know that nothing is guaranteed, and you have to put in the work. There is no guarantee that you can achieve a specific desired outcome; however, what is guaranteed is that you will have a negative result if you enter a negative situation with negative thoughts.

LIVE YOUR TRUTH!

OPRAH WINFREY AND VALERIE GOLDEN ALLEN

THE TRUTH SHALL SET YOU FREE!

VALERIE GOLDEN ALLEN

Sitting on the edge of my bed the night after my Mama's one-year transition from this place called earth, I wondered if she were watching over me like she said she would. All my life, she was there for me. That constant, through every storm or joyful occasion. Saying goodbye to your greatest supporter or cheerleader makes you wonder, who can I count on now aside from God? What are you left with as a woman in the 21st century when you think about who has your back? Hmmm...

Rubbing the small pea-like lump in my right breast seemed so unfair. Here I go again, darn! What a distraction as I thought of the fight we endured. My beautiful Sister, who was one year older, lost the battle to "BREAST CANCER" ten years ago, but here I am, fourteen years later, wondering why? Immediately, snatching myself back into reality, I murmured, "I trust you, God. Your word doesn't come back void, and You can't lie! You healed me, so enemy, you are defeated. I'm on the battlefield, but my God is with me!" In this season of my life, I've finally decided to face the "TRUTH" that whatever you allow to enter your mind and dwell on means the FATE is compromising your FAITH. Facing the "TRUTH" sometimes is not easy, especially when it comes to oneself. The mirror project has been around for a very long time. Whether hearing it from the person behind the podium in church, your therapist, your significant other, or oneself, the image staring back at you can be startling. Putting on your face every day of your life to show the world you're okay because you are a strong woman and cannot display pain can be so draining. Why do we do it? Why can't we be like others and not care? How do we save ourselves from ourselves? Well, my "TRUTH" is this constant battle in my mind that I'm supposed to be different. You know, being perfectly imperfect has its vices. What I put out has to mirror my actions because of whose watching and that I owe something even though I'm flawed. Encouraging myself daily as I strive to thrive in life has helped me face her. Those chains and shackles that try to keep me bound because of my shortcomings have to give way to release because of my stance on "TRUTH" to power! No more blaming myself for other folk's actions when they don't listen! I am no more trying to save something that doesn't want to be saved! No more will I dim my light to appease haters who despise my shine! And lastly, No more wondering if I will ever be accepted or good enough! Maya Angelou said it all in the phrase, "When people show you who they are, believe them the first time." Although I was taught in my adolescent years by my Grandma the "everyone deserves a second chance" motto, she reminded me that "God is a God of many chances. He is merciful and forgiving, and the Bible says you should forgive others seventy times seven." As I matured, I started doing the math and one day questioned her, "Why do I have to give them four hundred and ninety times to wrong me? I don't think I can do it, Grandma!"

She looked at me, astonished, with loving eyes and let out a little chuckle. Somehow, I believe she understood what I was saying. I love and respect her, but this bird isn't caged anymore! She's free! Free to be whoever and whatever she chooses to be! There is this freedom in be. To be good, to be naughty. To be at my best, to be lazy. To be creative, to be curious. To be silly, to be sassy. To be faithful or to be foolish. Now, with that said, what does all of it mean? It's my choice, isn't it to BE freakin' me in any way, shape, or fashion? So, now that I finally made peace with her and spewed my "TRUTH," I believe it's time to stand up and share my divine power for the greater good with those stuck. Helping them define their purpose and tapping into it has to be the prerequisite to being set free. You know, there is a price you must pay for freedom? I'm not alluding to being whipped with straps by Master, but by being beat, smoothed out, and pruned to get rid of those dead things stumping your growth. I believe in this season, there is an awakening taking place amongst women.

The good word "I once was lost, but now I'm found" is so profound! As some face their "TRUTH," they search for critical information to bring healing to their heart, mind, body, and soul. They crave insight through prayer, meditation, therapy, yoga, and messages of inspiration. They await opportunities to expose deep root causes that have kept them bewildered, crippled, and chained. This road called "life" isn't easy. We have harmed ourselves in many ways, which has caused deviation along our journey and a loss of sight to true purpose. Of course, there will be bumps, hiccups, and detours, but we can lessen our challenges and disappointments if our GPS is focused. This season, we must be intentional and resilient in fulfilling our call to destiny by casting down vain imaginations and hushing the voices in our minds that cause us to lose sight of the finished product. Devil! You are a liar; as I walked through the doors of Cleveland Clinic to face "The Truth" about the lump. Looking around the Imaging area, I felt a nervousness that filled the air with uneasiness. On many faces, I saw anxiety. The Hispanic woman sitting across from me was beet red as she wiped the flow of tears from her eyes. Silently, I interceded with prayer for her and every woman in that waiting area. I stood tall when they called my name and followed the nurse into the ultrasound room. Taking off my top and wrapping my body in the white cloth robe that she handed to me was a moment of "Truth." Again, I mummer, "I am pure, clean; I am cancer free; no matter what that machine or Doctor says, I still believe you, God." It was relatively warm as she squeezed the gel all over my upper body.

Back and forth, left to right, around and around, she moved the wand, trying to detect the silent sounds of the waves. If she tells me to get dressed, that means I'm good. Suddenly, I remembered the same test years ago and knew the routine. If told to stay, they must go further. She turned in the swivel chair, faced me, and said, "Ma'am, you must stay because the doctor needs to speak with you." I don't know, but I do know this; as I encouraged myself, God will put no more on you than you can bear. Stand Woman Stand! Trust Him no matter what! Suddenly, the phone rang, and although I didn't speak Spanish, I knew a few of the words. She said, "Ahi Que Linda! And, Si, then Nada," I knew that last word meant NO. The radiologist told me to dress and that my Oncologist would contact me in two or three days.

On the ride home, I decided to stop at Crackle Barrel and treat myself to breakfast. The pancakes with syrup were something I had been craving for months as I savored the syrup and enjoyed the slices of ole-fashion bacon. When the friendly waitress handed me the bill, I felt my phone vibrate in my cross-body purse in my lap. Who is this? It's too early in the morning to talk; this is my time of peace after all, I've been through lately. When I looked at my phone and saw two messages from the hospital, I thought, "they must want me to come back for something." I felt calm as I read my messages through the two-step verification process. The first message said scar tissue, benign. Yes, Lord! I yelled. Okay, calm down, Valerie; you have one more to go. I sighed and exhaled, not moving my eyes off the screen.

Suddenly, the message opened, stating a tiny 3-centimeter cyst, benign. Glory to the Highest!!! I stood on "The Truth" and trusted God no matter what it looked or felt like! My Heavenly Father truly is a Keeper! I'm Cancer Free! Being a lover of music, I searched for a song with words that would describe what I was feeling. A piece that is a setting free of oneself. One that you make peace with and give way to newness. To believe and say, "I am Amazing; I am Beautiful; I am a reflection of God's "TRUTH!" In my search, I found buried treasure in the song "I wish I knew how it will feel to be FREE" by Nina Simone. The life-changing words in the verse, "I wish I could give all I'm longing to give. I wish I could live like I'm longing to live. I wish I could do all the things that I can, and though I'm overdue, I'd be starting anew." Oops, there's that second chance, my Grandma spoke.

Looking over my life, I discovered I gave too much power to my rearview mirror. As lifelong learners, we must keep up with new trends and be open to learning something new and changing. It's evident none of us have it all together. Shifting my focus from the rearview to the big windshield in front of me was revitalizing. My soul, my soul, is being set free as I pen these words! Most of the time, when we share our viewpoints, one-on-one or in an audience of some, that finger points back at us. Discovering self-worth, self-image, self-determination, and, more importantly, self-love calls for self-analysis and being transparent with self. Do you want to be honest and "BE" all you are to be? Do you want to be set free and stand in your "TRUTH" no matter the judgment? Woman, are you ready to stand on "FAITH," not "FATE," and do the darn thing?

My friend, I want you to be delivered, set free, and "BE" all you were created to BE! Do you want to be delivered and don't give a "FREAKIN" you know what to the status quo? I need you to believe in yourself, my Sister. I need you to trust yourself and forgive the woman in the mirror. I need you to be "TRUTHFUL" even if you stand alone. Lastly, I need you to believe in God and know He is the Author and Finisher of your Fate and will never leave you.

YOUR DEEPEST THOUGHTS

Which "Truth" can you relate to?

_____

_____

_____

_____

What will you do now that you've faced the Truth?

_____

_____

_____

_____

What plan of action will you develop to move forward as you walk
in your Truth?

_____

_____

_____

_____

_____

_____

_____

LET "OUR" TRUTH BE TOLD, an anthem for women worldwide to wake up and face their **TRUTH**. Finding the courage to approach the reflection in the mirror is not easy. But you must in order to be unshackled and set free. Arise, **WOMAN**, and light your candle; the wick is not all gone. You have a purpose, you are significant, and yes, you matter! Fight for her! After reading these **TRUTHS** and believing in her, life will take another form. So, grab your passport, travel around the globe, and hear the voices on these pages as they share their **TRUTHS**.

Valerie Golden Allen is the author of several books, including the best-selling STAND WOMAN STAND! She is the Founder and President of the SWS Worldwide Movement. An Educator, Motivational Speaker, Life Coach, and Business Owner. She serves on several boards locally and nationwide. This native of Miami, Florida, is a Mother of four adult children and six amazing grandchildren.

www.ingramcontent.com/pod-product-compliance
Lightning Source LLC
Chambersburg PA
CBHW041930090426
42744CB00016B/1998